FOLLOW

A 30-DAY DEVOTIONAL
TO ENCOURAGE YOUR LIFE

Mike Sternad

FOLLOW
A 30-DAY DEVOTIONAL TO ENCOURAGE YOUR LIFE

By Mike Sternad

Published by Contented Life Publishing

Mailing Address: 312 T Schillinger Rd. S,
Mobile, Alabama 36608

Website: www.calvarychapelmobile.com
Email: mikesternad@gmail.com

Copyright © 2020 by Mike Sternad

Second edition.

All rights reserved. No part of this publication may be reproduced, stored in a retrieval system, or transmitted in any form or by any means without the express written consent of Mike Sternad.

Unless otherwise indicated, Scripture quotations in this book are taken from the New King James Version of the Bible. Copyright © 1979, 1980, 1982 by Thomas Nelson, Inc., Publishers. Used by permission.

Edited by Miriam Rogers
Cover Design by Ashley Garcia
Interior Design by Ulrika Towgood

ISBN 978-1-7343454-2-1

Printed in the United States of America

This book is dedicated to
my beautiful wife and my two amazing daughters.
You bring me so much joy in this life.
I am a blessed husband and father.

TABLE OF CONTENTS

FOREWORD		7
INTRODUCTION		9
DAY 1	**DO NOT WORRY**	13
DAY 2	**KINGDOM WORK**	16
DAY 3	**SERVING GOD**	19
DAY 4	**FOLLOW HIM**	23
DAY 5	**OPEN HANDS**	26
DAY 6	**AT THE DOOR**	29
DAY 7	**NO FEAR**	32
DAY 8	**FOCUS FORWARD**	35
DAY 9	**RELAY REALITY**	38
DAY 10	**BE JOYFUL**	41
DAY 11	**GIVE**	44
DAY 12	**GOD'S WORD**	47
DAY 13	**OUR HOME**	50
DAY 14	**PRAY OFTEN**	53
DAY 15	**TRUE VALUE**	56

TABLE OF CONTENTS (Continued)

DAY 16 **HEARING GOD** 59

DAY 17 **SUFFERING** 62

DAY 18 **FEAR AND FAITH** 65

DAY 19 **REACH OUT** 68

DAY 20 **HAVE COMPASSION** 71

DAY 21 **HEED GOD** 74

DAY 22 **BE AWARE** 77

DAY 23 **SURRENDERED** 80

DAY 24 **GOD'S WILL** 83

DAY 25 **RESIST** 86

DAY 26 **GOD'S HOUSE** 89

DAY 27 **RESCUED** 93

DAY 28 **PRAYING WITH FAITH** 96

DAY 29 **KINGDOM BUSINESS** 99

DAY 30 **GO ALL OUT** 102

CONCLUSION 105

FOREWORD

Follow.

How simple.

Mike Sternad refuses to weary us with complicated approaches that demand complex journeys through theological depths and conflicting ideas. No, this road travels straight, following the simple path that a child might understand. No getting lost. No invitation to argue.

So how does he do it? Jesus said to follow Him, and this book does it. No wandering down dead-end lanes. No backing up and trying again. No question about where you are and where you are going. If you are having trouble following Jesus, hurry up and read this book. It is mercifully short—a month's worth of devotional reading—and never leaves Scripture. You can't get lost and … you might even get found.

Amazing.

Enjoy.

> Gayle D. Erwin
> Author of *The Jesus Style*
> Servant Quarters
> Cathedral City, California

INTRODUCTION

"All Scripture is given by inspiration of God, and is profitable for doctrine, for reproof, for correction, for instruction in righteousness, that the man of God may be complete, thoroughly equipped for every good work." (2 Timothy 3:16-17)

I wasn't even a Christian and I was reading the Gospel of Matthew. What was I thinking? Why in the world was I being weird and reading the Bible when I didn't grow up in church and didn't care about all that God stuff? Looking back, I realize that I was seriously searching for truth because I was empty and void of any fulfillment or joy! I tried to find fulfillment in many different places with no positive outcome. After every worldly pursuit, I was left empty and unhappy. So when someone gave me a big NIV (New International Version) Study Bible, I just started reading the Gospel of Matthew—and I was absolutely amazed! All those deep questions I had about life were answered as I went through this book of the Bible. The red letters really jumped out at me and I was astounded at how Jesus spoke and dealt with people. He was loving, yet direct; comforting, yet corrective; honest, yet kind. After a couple months of reading the Bible, I began walking with the Lord and the rest is history. But it all started with the Word of God.

The entire Word of God is imperative to our spiritual growth. God spoke through His people in order to bring His Word into existence. As we get into God's Word, we are to let it get into our heads, hearts and lives. God's Word should permeate who we are and cause in us a desire to hear the truth and then put it into practice! In order to grow and thrive in our relationship with the Lord, digging into God's decrees is so incredibly essential. The way that the Lord has grown my faith was to let His Word get into my heart and mind! I have grown spiritually because of daily digging into the Scriptures and opening my heart for God to speak to me.

The whole counsel of God is important. Paul the apostle said in Acts 20:27, "For I have not shunned to declare to you the whole counsel of God." We don't hold certain parts of Scripture above other parts of Scripture, nor do we dismiss any portion of the Bible. We do not add to the Word of God, nor do we take away from the Scriptures. The whole Word of God is important, powerful and life-changing.

One of the studies that I've always loved doing is simply reading the words of Jesus. The statements He made, the questions He asked and answered, and the overall tactful way He had with words can teach us how to deal with confrontation and interaction. Jesus asked questions and answered questions. He made truth statements to the crowds and to individuals. He always spoke a word in season and ministered through the conversations He had.

In this devotional I've chosen to expound upon thirty Scriptures from the words of Jesus and I pray this devotional would encourage you in your walk with God. As you read God's Word, remember Who is speaking and let the words sink into your heart and mind. God wants to speak to you through His inspired Word and if we remain pliable and teachable, we will continue to learn and grow for the rest of our days here on planet Earth! As God speaks, may we listen.

> *"But He said, 'More than that, blessed are those who hear the word of God and keep it!'"* (Luke 11:28)

Mike Sternad
Pastor, Calvary Chapel Mobile, Alabama

DAY 1
DO NOT WORRY

"Therefore I say to you, do not worry about your life, what you will eat or what you will drink; nor about your body, what you will put on. Is not life more than food and the body more than clothing?" (Matthew 6:25)

Jesus does not want you to worry about those necessities that are required for you to live.

Worrying is such a waste of time. I look back and realize that most of what I worried about did not even come to pass! Have you ever worried like crazy over a hypothetical situation that it tore you down? I have too. Let's not do that anymore. Don't ever let worry wreck you or cause you to flounder in your faith. If you allow it, worry will lead to a loss of productivity and an insurmountable amount of stress. God did not create you to worry or be afraid about the present or the future. You don't have to worry about how the Lord will provide for you or how you will get through another day. You were never meant to live an unsettled life where you're in constant fear that your necessities won't be provided for. God has created you to live boldly for Him with a settled heart and an assured outlook. God has and will continue to provide for you!

Statistically, there is nothing beneficial about worrying. Being afraid can actually distract us from what truly matters in this life! How much have we missed out on because we were too busy being anxious about things that could possibly happen? It's like worrying so much about what could happen to your child that you don't actually enjoy the time you're spending with your child. One of my sisters had to get a separate health insurance policy for one of her sons because he loved to be a daredevil and do crazy stunt man actions and jump off high places—but that's a different story. Even then, worry isn't or shouldn't be justified. The faith within you should cause boldness and courage to flow out of you. Allowing worry to invade your mind will cause anxiety that will distract you and break you down and make you forget those things that you should remember. Worry will cause you to miss the moment; so instead of enjoying it, you are anxious through it. Events from the past can conjure up stress that is physically and spiritually unhealthy. The result of looking back at your life will cause major regret. Jesus makes it clear that we are not to waste our time worrying when we can be completely carefree. Take heed to Jesus' words and focus on the freedom that you have from Him!

> **Enjoy the moments you are in and kick worry to the curb.**

Jesus said not to worry about the details of your life and don't stress about being provided for! How much time have you spent just going crazy because you weren't sure how you were going to pay for this or that? Pray about it but don't be anxious. Of course, don't be negligent, but also don't go to the extreme in your mind and freak out about what God wants to give you peace about. In every season of life, where God guides and leads you, He will provide for you in every way! The Lord will feed and clothe us.

There have been times where I worry about finances and about how I will make it through the month. There have been times where all I could see was what I didn't have, rather than focusing on what God has blessed me with. I am done with worrying about things that are beyond my control. We must remember that the Lord has our lives in His hands. Therefore, we have no need to worry as we keep our eyes upon Jesus. This isn't some redundant cliché or something we have to recite repeatedly as Christians. This is reality! Worry is washed away when we are confident that the Lord will come through in all our situations and circumstances.

Be assured that the Lord is your peace through every single predicament. He is your rest and your relief! When your focus is on Him, worry will be nonexistent. God is sovereign and He is in control of it all, especially when things seem undone. God's got you and me. Burdens will be a thing of the past as you totally trust in the Lord for provision. Start living the way God intended you to live—with a settled heart and peace of mind.

DAY 2
KINGDOM WORK

> *Jesus said to them, "My food is to do the will of Him who sent Me, and to finish His work."* (John 4:34)

When you understand that you have a divine purpose to live out, your heart will be full and satisfied. Walking on the path of God's purpose for you is the best place to be! The clear key to living in the center of God's mission is to hear and heed the Lord on a daily basis. When you are led by the Lord and live for the Lord, you'll find yourself on the divine adventure God orchestrates for you specifically. Embrace it and enjoy it!

The consistent goal in this life is to be about our Father's business. Before He began His public ministry, Jesus, being our example, made it clear what life is about! How long did you live your life attempting to find happiness in everything other than the Lord? I spent many years trying everything I could to be fulfilled and satisfied. I kept ending up empty and alone. Then as I searched for truth, God showed up and changed everything! We are not here to just live and die, we are here to fulfill God's will with the time God has given us!

Food nourishes and fulfills a desire in our body. There are times when we are so hungry we become lightheaded, cranky and off-balance. Our stomachs are in pain and we long to eat. It does not matter what we eat, we just need sustenance quickly! After we eat some food, we smile again, are clear-headed and regain energy. If you're a parent, you know that food is super necessary to live and sustain human life and be sane. We need to eat to live! In the same way, doing God's work nourishes our soul and is necessary to fulfill God's will. Spiritual hunger dissipates as we pursue God's plans for us. As God sends us out to fulfill our calling and enact His plans for eternity, we are called to simply follow Him. The more we consistently serve the Lord, the more we realize that satisfaction stems only from walking in God's will for us.

> You can live your whole life in want or you can live your life for Jesus and be totally fulfilled.

Oftentimes we start a multitude of tasks and projects and do not complete them. Halfway through we completely forget about the project and it sits in the garage untouched and unfinished. When it comes to the work of the Lord, our aim should be to finish our God-given goals and follow through on God's purposes for us. When God calls us to something, may we, with our whole heart, complete that God-given task.

I've had to tell people they can't serve in a ministry because they don't finish what they start or they half-heartedly serve the Lord, seeing it more as a volunteer role rather than a service unto the living God. I'll never forget when a woman from Calvary Chapel LAX was cleaning the church every week. I was so thankful, and so one day I said to her, "Thank you so much for regularly cleaning the church!" She replied without hesitation, "I'm not doing it for you, I'm doing it for the

Lord!" That answer did not offend me but instead it blessed me like crazy! That is the heart to have! Everything we do is unto and for the Lord! When God leads us in a certain direction, we do not want to leave it undone or unfinished. Just as God wants to finish the work He began in you, we should desire to finish the work He's given us to do!

May your goal be to complete God's calling every day and in each season of your life. Continually depend upon the Lord and seek Him for what He wants you to do, where He wants you to go, and who He wants you to talk to. As you connect and communicate with God about His plans for you and walk in His will, the result will be true purpose and real fulfillment. You exist to do kingdom work. You are not living for yourself. God gives you a goal and a purpose. Ask for His wisdom and strength to live out what He has called you to do. It is such a privilege to serve the Lord and further His kingdom. All glory to Him!

DAY 3
SERVING GOD

"Blessed is that servant whom his master will find so doing when he comes." (Luke 12:43)

If you are walking with God, you are in His will. It's really that simple! If you are following Jesus, He will direct you in the way you should go and make His plans clear to you. You are not called to be idle until the Lord gives you "a sign from heaven" to get up and get going. The Lord will supernaturally lead you in very natural ways. Be active in living for God and watch Him work! We don't have to constantly search for God's will our whole lives as if He were hiding it from us. The Lord's will for His kids is that we simply follow His Word and seek Him through prayer.

When I was a new believer, I was at a home Bible study and the pastor gave each person small slips of paper, each with a verse on it. On mine was written Jeremiah 29:11 which says, "For I know the thoughts that I think toward you, says the LORD, thoughts of peace and not of evil, to give you a future and a hope." This has been a verse that I've lived by for years and it reminds me that as long as I am in the middle of God's mission for me, I'm in His will and He has work for me to do. I realized early on that I don't have to try and be strategic to figure out His will every single day. I just have to consistently follow Him and know that as I submit to His leading, I am in His will now and in the future.

God's general will is a blessing as we take the truth in and then go out and spread the truth whenever and wherever we can! Life is about our relationship with the Lord first and with others second. If we are putting God first in our lives, then our connection to Him will spill over to our relationships and connection with others. It's not about our tribe first, it's about our time with the Lord first. The more we know His heart, the more our hearts will want to reach out to others with love from above. If we are hearing from God through prayer and His Word, then we are both relationally connected to God and gaining directives from Him. We are in the Lord's general will if we are being obedient; we are in His specific will if we are actively connected and in communication with Him. He gives us promises, we take them in, wait on Him, and then He fulfills those promises! Charles Spurgeon, an English preacher from the nineteenth century, said, "One of the greatest rewards that we ever receive for serving God is the permission to do still more for Him." How amazing and exciting it is to be actively serving the Lord on this earth!

Being active for the kingdom of God is an amazing blessing.

The only way you can see your specific purpose from season to season is to be moving forward in your faith. We are called to grow from milk to meat, as the Bible says. In other words, we learn the foundational truth

---

Spurgeon, Charles. *The Complete Works of C. H. Spurgeon, Volume 48: Sermons 2760 to 2811*. https://books.google.com/books?id=n7FcCgAAQBA-J&dq=Spurgeon+one+of+the+greatest+rewards+that+we+ever+receive&source=gbs_navlinks_s

from the Word of God, and then as we grow in our faith we go deeper and deeper into those truths. As we follow the Lord, He is the only One who can make our purpose clear. This is why it's so critical to stay in constant communication with God instead of depending on people's perspectives first. Yes, God can and has used people in my life to confirm things and direct me, but they come second to God's leading.

We are privileged to implement His directives in our lives. But if we are not actively seeking God, we may throw up our hands in frustration wondering why we are not hearing from Him. We may ask, *What did I do wrong? Why aren't You there for me?!* The reality is we will hear nothing when we are being passive in our faith rather than being active in our faith! We are frustrated because we want to know God's will, but we are not asking, seeking, or knocking (Matthew 7:7). We are not called to be sideline saints or the *frozen chosen*. We are called to get up and get going in the name of the Lord and do His work, which is work with a purpose.

Make it a priority to stay closely connected to your amazing Creator. He wants you to call upon Him on a daily basis. May you not only speak to Him, may you have ears to hear what He directs you to do! Be obedient to God and simply follow Him. Abide in the Lord who absolutely loves you and wants you to live out His plan for you. You will daily fulfill God's will as you let Him go before you. Don't ever jump ahead of the Lord, instead let Him lead. He knows the ins and outs of your journey and He knows your destination from season to season. Keep close communication with the Lord for He longs to hear from you and direct you!

DAY 4
FOLLOW HIM

> When He had called the people to Himself, with His disciples also, He said to them, "Whoever desires to come after Me, let him deny himself, and take up his cross, and follow Me." (Mark 8:34)

As you meditate on this verse, it will remind you what life as a believer is all about. Jesus' words are a call to action. They will challenge you, convict you, and exhort your heart. Jesus cuts through all the sugar-coated religious talk and gets straight to the point.

Following Jesus requires three important actions. The first is denying self. This does not mean you cease to have fun or stop spending time on things you enjoy. Denying self means surrendering ourselves to Christ and obeying His will; no longer living to satisfy our carnal and fleshly desires that emanate from a sin-filled outlook. Yes, you still take care of yourself, brush your teeth, take a shower and put deodorant on. Take care of yourself but don't be consumed with yourself. Self-absorption is commendable in our American culture but it's disgusting to God.

The second action is to take up your cross. The cross was an instrument of death, a one-way ticket to execution with no way back. Sounds pretty intense, right? But taking up your cross means you are whole-heartedly and unashamedly following Jesus—that it costs something to follow Jesus, but the cost is worth the sacrifice. Paul said, "I die daily" (1 Corinthians 15:31). But we don't believe in reincarnation, so what did he mean? Paul died to his own desires and instead lived for the Lord's desires. This mindset pleases the Lord.

The third action that a person must take for a commitment to Jesus is to simply follow Him. It sounds simple enough, but it really can be extremely difficult. Following Jesus will cause a person to abandon their self-led life and begin to be led by the Spirit. This isn't always an easy transition. At first, I had a tough time peeling away from the world and following Jesus. I was learning what following Jesus meant and what I had to do. It was tough breaking away from people I thought were friends but who influenced me in negative and ungodly ways. It was difficult, but it was worth it because it all became part of my spiritual growth experience. Following Jesus will force a person to break away from those things that kept them away from Jesus in the past. It may be painful at first, but it leads to freedom!

> **To intentionally follow Jesus is to surrender on a regular basis.**

Follow Me—acting on these two words of Jesus can change your whole destiny. When Jesus called believers to follow Him, it truly sounded simple, but it was far from easy. Following Jesus means we are done following our own plans for ourselves, which can be hard for those who are used to doing things their own way, on their own terms and in their own time. Sometimes we can be so tightfisted with our plans that there is no room for God to intervene and change what He wants to change. Following Jesus means we have surrendered our surface dreams for something so much deeper, greater and more amazing. Following Jesus means we are set free and we are secure in the hands of God. Following Jesus means our purpose is realized, and His plans for us are clear as we walk by faith. It is such a privilege and so amazing to be a follower of Jesus Christ. There is nothing like it in this world! I find it so adventurous to walk by faith as I am led by God. I am pleasantly overwhelmed at the fact that as believers we get to follow the God of the universe.

Put both feet into the Father's will and see God radically move the mountains that you thought were a blockade. What you see as a roadblock is actually God making a roadway so you can continue to move forward in the faith. As you place Him first, your priorities will be in order. Taking these three actions can activate the faith inside of you and bring you into a deeper and more profound life in Christ.

DAY 5

OPEN HANDS

"Give to him who asks you, and from him who wants to borrow from you do not turn away."
(Matthew 5:42)

Be a giver. Don't let what you possess, possess you. When it comes to the material, have open hands all the time and don't have an iron grip on those things that rust and decay. The reality is that you don't own anything, it is all God's! Remember to place value not on things in this world but on the eternal things. You are not called to be a taker; you are called to be a giver of what God has given you.

Everything we have is on loan from the Lord. We often place value on objects that will never bring lasting contentment or happiness. Can Apple please stop coming out with new and updated iPads so quickly! It temps me and makes me think I'm missing out if I don't buy the latest technology with all the new capabilities. Yet, those things aren't the end-all of happiness; they are just tools to be used for the Lord. Most of what we have and collect only has value because we ascribe value to them. The truth is that God is valuable and of *utmost* importance in this life, not stuff. As we pursue Him and walk with Him, we see that we are fulfilled and He is all we need. May we ascribe value to the Lord and those spiritual blessings that come from above.

This life is not about accumulating stuff in an attempt to feel secure. As Christians we are not supposed to be characterized as people who just take, take, take! We are called to be givers just like Jesus was while on this earth! Jesus never promoted hoarding, nor does He applaud believers who build little material kingdoms on this earth. Generally speaking, our attitude should be that of giving and we should be focused on others daily. There is no room for stinginess in the life of a saint, nor is there room for greediness or covetousness. Life is too short to accumulate a bunch of stuff that only brings temporary satisfaction. Jesus is telling us to give to those who truly have need in this life. The greatest way we can fulfill the needs of others is to share the heart of God with them so that their emptiness will be filled!

The Lord rejoices when we hold onto our stuff lightly, and yet hold on to Him with the grip of genuine faith! Continue to pursue God rather than pursuing items that the world deems valuable. God is valuable. His Word is valuable. Getting the gospel out is valuable. Focus on this mindset and know that every single thing you have is from God!

> Having open hands means we do not place high value on stuff, but instead we place high value on the spiritual.

We are not to be *needs* driven; we are to be *calling* driven. There will always be deep-seated needs in this world, but you and I cannot fill them all! But we have to seek God to know what or who He wants us to reach out to.

Everything we do should be doused and flooded with prayer before we make any decision and take action. Jesus preached to the crowds and helped and healed those whom the Father called Him to help and heal. May we be in tune with the Lord so we know who we can reach out to.

God wants you to realize how overwhelmingly blessed you actually are. He gives good gifts to His kids. Have a giving mentality and relay the heart of God to those in need, those who are down and in despair. Give the gospel to those who are in want and feel alone. May generosity be a habit that you practice in your everyday life even as Jesus continually gave throughout His whole ministry. May you have open hands when it comes to helping others. After all, He has given to us everything we need for life and godliness (2 Peter 1:3).

DAY 6
AT THE DOOR

"Behold, I stand at the door and knock. If anyone hears My voice and opens the door, I will come in to him and dine with him, and he with Me."
(Revelation 3:20)

There was a time when the Lord Jesus knocked on the door of your heart. You heard it and you may have resisted initially, but you eventually opened the door and let Him in. The door closed behind you and you realized you were chosen before the foundation of the world. Jesus loves you and He is so incredibly blessed that you are walking with Him! The angels rejoiced when you began your walk with the Lord. As you continue to live for Jesus, the tendency is to forget that He is in your heart and sometimes act like He is outside of your life. You've let Him in, now it's time to daily let Him clean house and have His way.

In today's verse, Jesus is telling the lukewarm church that there is a way to have a deep personal relationship with Him. Back in that day, when you dined with someone it was a warm, blessed and intimate experience. It wasn't just a casual meal at Chick-fil-A with friends while your kids played in the play area. Dining together was a time of closeness and conversation. As we let the Lord in, the result will be a closeness to Him and the opportunity to commune with Him. The fact that Jesus is with us and hears our prayers is pretty mind blowing!

Jesus changes our hearts and transforms our outlook. Before I was saved I didn't even realize my outlook needed to be altered! Yet as I lived for the Lord He renewed my mind and changed my desires (Romans 12:1-2). I began to learn from the Bible, and from more mature Christians who knew the Bible, how to live and what my mission was as a believer. I quickly realized that Jesus wants to turn lukewarm complacency into fiery passion. When you open the door of your heart to Jesus, you are inviting Him to come in and change everything.

> The Lord Jesus never tries to break down the door, He politely and peacefully knocks on the door. Let Him in.

This verse applies to both sinner and saint. If you are unsaved, open your heart to Jesus and watch Him radically work in your life. I did and it has been an amazing adventure and a blessed ride. If you are saved but are lukewarm, invite Jesus into your heart's home and develop your personal relationship with Him. Don't let miracles become monotonous to you and don't let the fact that you've been delivered become dull. It is not easy to be a follower of Jesus, but it is the *best* thing in the world! I've met believers who act like Eeyore! They always seem down and don't know what a bright side is, and I just don't understand that. I mean, I get that we all go through and face trials, but we are saved, set apart for heaven, and are on a journey through God's will. May we constantly rejoice!

The whole point of this passage is to open the door to Jesus and let Him in! He doesn't bring discouragement or burdens to bear, He brings peace, rest, purpose and joy. Notice that Jesus doesn't forcibly break down the door in an attempt to invade a life. He does not try to find a way in the home against the homeowner's will, nor does He have tools that He uses to break in and make you believe. Jesus knocks on the door and allows us to answer the door willingly. May we not leave Jesus out of our heart's home. May we let Him in to do heart cleaning and life transformation.

Daily we have opportunity to open the door to a deep and profound relationship with the Lord. Make every morning a starting point where you let the Lord lead your life. Draw near to the Lord and allow yourself to be vulnerable toward how God wants to work in you. You will fall more and more in love with the Lord as you consistently let Him into every part of your life. Hear His voice and respond to Him and your life will never be the same. You will never regret it.

DAY 7

NO FEAR

> *Now the Lord spoke to Paul in the night by a vision, "Do not be afraid, but speak, and do not keep silent; for I am with you, and no one will attack you to hurt you; for I have many people in this city."* (Acts 18:9-10)

Don't be afraid for there is no need to fear. Whatever and wherever the Lord has called you presently, He will equip you in every way. The Lord will assure you and calm your heart during those times when you are somewhat anxious and unsettled. Even if your situation looks impossible and even if your heart is a bit timid about what God is calling you to do, just know that you can completely depend on Him for courage and boldness.

God does not speak to His children randomly. In today's verse, Jesus said not to be afraid because Paul was fearful! Even though he clearly had great faith he wasn't immune to fear. Sometimes I will be reading one of Paul's thirteen epistles in the New Testament and I think about how perpetually courageous he was! Yet, he had his moments where the Lord needed to reassure and remind him there is no need to fear. Sometimes we need those extra assurances from God that He is holding us and keeping us safe.

I pray a little more when I travel throughout the country. I don't pray because I'm paranoid, I pray for assurance from the Lord that my heart would be settled as I take off into the air of uncertainty. I actually like flying and traveling but when I do, I want to make sure I have peace and rest from the Lord since traveling can be stressful and nerve-racking. I'll never forget that scene in *Home Alone* where the family is running frantically through the airport trying to catch their flight. It was chaos. The fact is, as we are living for the Lord, there may be times when we start to overthink a situation and we begin to doubt or we don't see how we will get through. We must always remember that God is our active refuge! He has us and holds us. The Bible tells us that God is our strong tower and our hiding place. Therefore, fear is not allowed to have a foothold upon our lives.

> Communicate with the Lord during those times where you feel unsure and God will give you the assurance you need.

As believers we need to band together because unity results in strength. We can only do so much on our own, but when we stick together as Christians we can accomplish a ton of eternal work. Yes, God protects us, but we are to be involved in each other's lives as well. We are called to pray for one another, keep each other accountable, and hold each other up like Aaron and Hur did for Moses during a major battle (see Exodus 17:12-14). This war was won because the people joined together to fight against the enemy. This is what we have the privilege of doing as the body of Christ. We know that our source of security is the Lord Jesus Christ. We need Him for clarity, wisdom and strength. At the same time, God has created us to connect and be cohesive in this life. God has people in every city and He brings believers together as they minister and reach out to this lost world.

I love meeting believers from all over the world because it reminds me that we are in this fight of faith together. We are never alone because our heavenly Father is with us, but we also have brothers and sisters in Christ who are active in kingdom work as well! Sure, many are called but few are chosen, but there are more active Christian workers than you think! Please don't ever forget that you are not alone and you are in His hands—nobody can snatch you out of His hand (John 10:28).

You have to choose to let your fear fall by the wayside. Let your faith flourish and your heart burn with fiery passion to proclaim the truth to lost and confused souls. Don't be consumed with *what could* happen. Those *what if* questions are countenance killers and have no place in your life. Ask God to fill you so full of the Holy Spirit that anxiety is crowded out. Panic has no place in your heart for the peace of God is there for the taking. Let God destroy any distress that threatens to dampen your life or pull down your countenance. Forsake your fears. Let God be your active refuge. You can always run to Him for safety.

DAY 8
FOCUS FORWARD

Jesus said to him, "No one, having put his hand to the plow, and looking back, is fit for the kingdom of God." (Luke 9:62)

In order to make progress for the kingdom of God, do not look back—look ahead! Keep your eyes upon the course that God has set for you and continue on. The way to forge ahead on your journey is by fervently moving forward in the faith, keeping your eyes upon Jesus and your heart bent toward the Lord. Do not allow yourself to get dismayed or discouraged by what has happened; instead, be encouraged by what God is doing in and through your life right now.

When God saves and sanctifies us, we leave behind our old life and continue on in the new. In a sense, our old life dies and is buried and we rise up with a new heart and a new outlook in this world. The problem is when we get distracted by the things of the world and revert to our old way of thinking, our growth can be stunted.

In my Christian walk there had been times where the world's pull began to lure me away from church and the things of the Lord. I began to drift away, and my spiritual life suffered. I began to separate myself from the service I was doing for the Lord and I became miserable and discontented. May we not forget how empty it is to live for ourselves and may we never neglect the Lord and His work. When God says move forward, we must agree and go, instead of being like Lot's wife and looking back to how it used to be. Remember how before we began walking with God life was not fun or fulfilling? We were empty, alone, misguided and influenced by the ungodly ways of the world. If we are not intentionally walking with God, we will begin to think like the children of Israel who, after three days of freedom from Egypt, started complaining! They should have been thankful that they were free after all those years of bondage! Instead they forgot that God rescued them and they were no longer slaves. May we remember that God has freed us from the things of this world and set us on the path of His purposes. God not only saved our soul, He saved us from the way we used to live.

> You can praise God for He has saved you and has major purpose for your life.

Active faith means moving forward boldly instead of running backward in timidity. Maybe you are ultra goal-oriented; if you don't get things done you feel like a failure. I get you because I'm the same way! For those of us who are goal-oriented, we are blessed because the God of the universe has some work for us to do! Our purpose is given to us by the Lord, not by this world. We are not called to be conceited or boastful in what we've done for God's kingdom; He wants us to be humble.

To be fit for the kingdom does not mean we've reached some level of attainment or perfection—it means our faith is pointed forward and our eyes are upon the eternal, rather than the carnal. The only reason we should look to our past is to see how God has delivered us from those ensnaring sins. Leave the past behind and progress forward. Like the apostle Paul said in Philippians 3:13-14, "Brethren, I do not count myself to have apprehended; but one thing I do, forgetting those things which are behind and reaching forward to those things which are ahead, I press toward the goal for the prize of the upward call of God in Christ Jesus."

Keep your eyes upon Jesus, not on the former things. Otherwise, you may be lured back into your old way of thinking if you begin to romanticize about the past instead of remembering how miserable it was without Jesus in your life! Look ahead and know that God is pleased when you press on toward those goals He has set for you. Do not revisit your sordid past but press on toward the calling that God has for you. *Don't. Look. Back.*

DAY 9

RELAY REALITY

> *He answered and said to them, "You give them something to eat."* (Mark 6:37a)

God sees your need and what you go through. He cares when you struggle and is always there to help you every single day and every step of the way. God will direct you as you continue to step out in faith in the midst of God's mission. He desires for you to be calling-driven, not needs-driven. There will always be many needs and you cannot fulfill them all. Your calling is to meet those needs that the Lord is *calling you* to specifically fulfill. We cannot fulfill every need all the time, but God can.

God has a heart toward the brokenhearted and the poor. In the same way, may our hearts discern and recognize the needs of others instead of just focusing on ourselves all day long. We can tend to be so self-focused that we forget we are called to step out to help the hurting and share the gospel. Jesus saw the people who were hungry and provided for them—the disciples wanted to send the people away! The disciples were in the midst of learning what it looked like to have a heart to help people who felt helpless.

Remember that God doesn't look at the outward; He looks at the heart. Giving money doesn't count if your motivation is off. Doing good things won't please God if the reason is anything other than to bless the Lord.

As we seek God, He will give us compassion and a heart for the hurting.

The very things we don't want to deal with may be the very things God wants us to confront, so He can deal with us. Those problems that we try to pry away from may be the situations that God uses to work radically on our hearts. It's rarely convenient to put others above ourselves for we are innately sinful and selfish; yet that is what we are called to do. "Let each of you look out not only for his own interests, but also for the interest of others" (Philippians 2:4). The more I live my life for the Lord and for others, the more exciting and blessed life actually is! We are not called to take and be moochers in this life. We are called to unconditionally give.

> When you see those in need, don't see them as inconveniences; see them as opportunities to relay the reality of God's heart.

The Lord often used physical provision as a bridge to sharing spiritual truth. One time before I was a believer, the lock on my car wouldn't work so I called a locksmith to come out and fix it. This guy was talking to me about Jesus the whole time he was working on my lock! But as he was sharing the gospel with me, I truly saw that He believed in what he was saying, and it made me listen intently. Looking back, I realize the hand of God on that situation. God will use the natural to give glimpses of the supernatural. The Lord provides for the hurting and the hungry in order to help, but also as a means to share hope. In this verse, Jesus saw the physical need, but fulfilling that need was not the end in itself. Fulfilling that need was the means to see the spiritual realm and to share the hope that comes from above. We do not live for surface level things. We live for those deeper unseen things that affect and change our lives. As we are led by God, may we recognize the physical need, but attempt to share the spiritual fulfillment that can be had. The unseen spiritual realm is what we get to relay even as we help out in physical and material ways.

Every day you have the privilege to reach out with the good news of Jesus Christ. Put the interest of others above your own and don't be afraid to be uncomfortable for the sake of a soul being saved. Buy a meal for the hungry and use that action to share about the antidote to sin. When you share spiritual truth, it will help the needy and open their eyes to the supernatural. God is not interested in outward change; He is interested in inward transformation through the Word of God. The gospel is the answer to the need of humankind.

DAY 10
BE JOYFUL

But immediately Jesus spoke to them, saying, "Be of good cheer! It is I; do not be afraid."
(Matthew 14:27)

Fear is a faith stopper that prevents you from truly living for the Lord. Fear is a plague that can steal every ounce of hope and joy and leave you miserable. The way to combat fear and the key to joy is to believe these words of Jesus. He is with you; therefore, there is no room for fear to reside in your heart. You should be elated, excited and relieved because you have nothing to fear! The Lord Jesus is with you wherever you go and whatever you do. This truth should be enough for your timidity to be completely terminated. Knowing emphatically that the Lord will never leave you should give you a sense of courage, bravery and renewed strength.

Jesus is assuring these guys that they have no need to fear but every reason to be joyful! Fear will cause us to cower away in a corner and give up on what God is calling us to do. My closet at home doubles as a closet and storage room. There is literally no room to fit anything else in there even if I tried! So too, fear will have no room to reside in the heart that is filled with the Holy Spirit! Let God's presence hijack your fear and put to death worldly timidity. John tells us, "Perfect love casts out fear" (1 John 4:18). To *cast out* means to throw something far away from you—like my daughters do when they play the game called Hot Potato. You don't want to be caught holding that hot potato when the music stops, or you'll get hypothetically burned!

When we walk with God, the result is excitement and expectancy. The simple truth is that God is love and as He abides in our hearts, fear is cast out resulting in true joy! Sure, we are in a spiritual battle now that we are walking with the Lord, but the reality is that I've never been more joyful since I've been saved! When I gave no mind to the Lord Jesus and didn't care about spiritual things, I was empty. There was this void that no person or thing could fill. I would sit up late at night and just be fearful thinking about what would happen when I die. When I began my walk with the Lord, I was set free and forgiven and Jesus was now with me. I knew where I'd go when I died and I knew God would be with me while I lived.

> **When we actively acknowledge that God is with us, joy is integrated and fear is incinerated.**

We fear when we are unsure. In Matthew 14, the disciples were afraid because they didn't recognize Jesus as He was walking on the water at night. It was difficult to see who was coming toward them as they peered at the figure from the boat. It says, "Immediately Jesus spoke to them." Jesus wanted the disciples to know it was Him so their hearts would revert from being in terror to having peace. Jesus didn't play a game to see how long until they recognized Him, instead He immediately spoke when anxiety arose. As we live our lives as believers, we are comforted by the presence of

God and the Lord's still small voice. God impresses things upon our hearts and leads us through open and closed doors as we are sensitive to the Spirit and led by the Spirit. The more we live for the Lord, the more we can discern if the Lord is speaking to us or not. When we truly know Jesus is with us, we will be comforted by His voice and completely elated with joy.

No external circumstances should cause fear to well up inside of you. You have no need to fear because Jesus is with you and He always will be. May God's presence drive out any trepidation or anxiety that resides in your heart and mind. May His presence cause you to be completely free of fear and full of joy. Please remember that He is there in the darkness and in the storm. Take heart for He will get you through!

DAY 11
GIVE

> *I have shown you in every way, by laboring like this, that you must support the weak. And remember the words of the Lord Jesus, that He said, "It is more blessed to give than to receive."*
> (Acts 20:35)

You have God-given opportunities to help those in need. Those who are weak need the Lord's strength and you get to relay that the Lord is your source of strength when weariness sets in. Materially you can help, but really, what people need is to be woken up spiritually. As you live your life for God, you will see people exactly how Jesus saw people—with genuine compassion.

This verse is not talking about giving all your money to the church in faith. I hate that some churches use this very verse to make their services all about money, ripping people off. This verse is about focusing on the less fortunate and reaching out to those who truly need help. As believers, the weak should not be overlooked, marginalized or forgotten. When encountering a homeless man, C. S. Lewis took out his wallet and gave all his money. His friend said, "What are you doing giving him your money like that? Don't you know he's just going to squander it?" Lewis paused and replied, "That's all I was going to do with it."

The point is that our hearts should be prepared and ready to give whether it's time, resources, or the truth that God has called us to share! We have the privilege of lifting up those who are down and praying for those who are in a desperate place. We have the opportunity to be an encouragement to those who are helpless and give the gospel to those who are hopeless. Jesus recognized the weak and reached out to people who were at their end.

> Our great goal is to be others-centered rather than self-centered.

When we give, we are truly blessed. In our culture this sounds backwards because people have bought into the idea that the more we have, the better we feel about ourselves and the happier we become. That's not even close to being true. The most miserable people that I've met are those who have it all in the world's eyes. They have *no* peace and absolutely *no* joy. See, we were not created to take, take, take, nor are we called to be perpetual hoarders. We are blessed when we share with others our blessings. When we give, even in small ways, it hugely blesses those who are weak and in need.

The Word of God tells us that we have no need to be timid or shy away from reaching out. In Jeremiah 1:6-7, it says, "Then said I: Ah, Lord God! Behold, I cannot speak, for I am a youth." But the Lord said to me: Do not say, 'I am a youth,' for you shall go to all to whom I send you, and whatever I command you, you shall speak." Fear can stop the flow of blessings from us to others. May we be bold in our giving and in our sharing as we truly put others first. The very best gift we can give to those who are in need is Jesus. Possessions wear out, but the gift of the gospel is everlasting!

Actively seek out those in need and do something about it. Do not ignore those who have been ignored and overlooked their whole lives. Do not neglect those who are in desperate need of the Lord Jesus Christ. Reach out and give out instead of just taking. Resist selfishness and consumerism and make it a daily spiritual habit to look beyond your circumstances. Let the gospel be heralded from every area that God leads you to. Don't be a taker, be a giver. As Jesus clearly said in the context of the weak, "It is more blessed to give than to receive."

DAY 12
GOD'S WORD

But Jesus answered him, saying, "It is written, 'Man shall not live by bread alone, but by every word of God.'" (Luke 4:4)

The Bible is your source of spiritual health and your weapon. It is a weapon strong enough to fight against those nagging and intense temptations. It will prevent a teardown of your faith and bring truth to light so you can resist the lies of the enemy. With the Scriptures in your heart, you will halt the enemy's attempt to lure you away from your almighty God. As Jesus used the Scriptures in the desert during a time of weakness, so you too can use the Scriptures to fight against temptations that threaten to take you out.

Healthy food is filled with nutrients to give us the energy we need to sustain us. Food fills us up physically and usually fills us with comfort and much joy. The barbecue here in the South is so incredibly good! When we first moved here, I visited an establishment called Meat Boss about five times in the first three weeks. The restaurant is so true to its name because they have the best ribs, pulled pork and chicken around! They've won many awards, and you'll quickly understand why at first bite! I leave that place so incredibly satisfied and happy. So too with the Word of God. The Word of God leads to spiritual health for our soul and contains the heavenly nutrients that we need. As we consistently feed off of the Scriptures, we will deflect any and all temptations that we face.

In today's passage, Jesus used God's Word against the tempter as a defense not to give in to sin. Just as healthy food can deflect diseases, spiritual food can deflect unhealthy desires. God's Word helps us not to walk in the flesh and instead walk in the Spirit and live in line with God's ways. I don't want to be malnourished and unhealthy when it comes to my faith. I know about spiritual unhealthiness because at one time in my walk I was not consistently in the Word or praying or gathering together with other like-minded believers. My spiritual life staggered because I drifted off into the world and ceased to be intentional in seeking God! Honestly, I was left spiritually empty. Stick to God's Word so that even during those dry seasons when God seems silent, you can fall back on what you do know—He is still with you working. The result of using the Bible to fend off the darkness is complete victory! May we constantly have a balanced meal of truth in order to gain the strength and wisdom we need to fight the temptations that will be before us.

> **Spiritual health doesn't magically appear, it comes through consistently feeding off of the Word of God.**

Living this life as a Christian is no game, nor is it easy. It can be a battle as the unholy trinity—the world, the flesh and the devil—attempt to bring us down and take us out. If we don't have the Scriptures hidden in our hearts, then the temptations will become too much to bear and we'll end up giving in to sin over and over again. Sin is destructive and can become a vicious cycle if we don't engage in the battle with the weapons God has given us. One major way we resist major sin is to take care of our soul as we integrate God's Word into our hearts. Spiritual growth results from consistently being in God's Word and letting it into every facet of our lives. If Jesus used God's Word to protect against sin, how much more should we do the very same thing! Jesus was able to resist because He used God's Word as a weapon to defend against lies, corruption and darkness. May we not only read God's Word; may we use it from day to day to fend off the enemy's attacks and to stand firm in the truth!

Don't include a portion of the Bible into your spiritual diet, make it the main course! Your spiritual hunger will be met with fulfillment when you daily dig into the Scriptures, filling the deepest part of your life. Don't just read the Bible for head knowledge, read the Bible for heart transformation. God's Word is not dormant; it is living and active and speaks straight to your heart and meets you in your present circumstances. God's perfect Word will quench your spiritual thirst.

DAY 13

OUR HOME

"And if I go and prepare a place for you, I will come again and receive you to Myself; that where I am, there you may be also." (John 14:3)

Our true home is not here on earth; it is in heaven. We were not made for this world, and that is why we do not feel completely comfortable or at home here. We are temporarily camping on this fallen location called planet Earth. One day we will arrive at our true home where God is present and sin is absent. One day we'll take our last breath on this earth and our first breath in paradise where we will be completely at peace with no heartache, sorrow or pain.

Those who call on the name of the Lord are saved, and their home is being set up by the Lord. There are times when I would get caught up in those shows that my wife loves to watch where they take a beat up home and make it beautiful. There is not one episode where you are disappointed at the outcome because those who flipped the home did an amazing job! The Bible tells us that Jesus is fixing up our home and it is not on this earth; it is in heaven! Everything on earth is temporary, everything beyond is permanent. It's as if we are in a waiting room, expectant for our name to be called to see the Doctor, to be healed completely. We hear His voice, we hear our name being called, and we enter into the joy of the Lord.

Don't get too comfortable on this earth, attempting to find your security here. Sometimes we can live like this world is the place we're going to reside in forever. Not true! We are not called to set up our little kingdoms on earth and live our lives as comfortable as possible. We are simply passing through on the way to paradise. Find comfort and complete rest in the fact that you have a place waiting in heaven that is absent of anxiety, stresses and fears.

> We are passing through this earth on the way to our true home.

When we die, we are going to live with the Lord forever. That is not a disappointment; that is the best news ever! Heaven is not going to be amazing just because we will see other believers there; heaven is going to be amazing because we'll be with Jesus for eternity! The more you draw near to Him on this earth, the more you'll realize how amazing He is and the more you'll fall in love with Him. When we find fulfillment in the Lord while living on this earth, we will long to be with Him in heaven! He satisfies every area of our lives. Heaven is not a boring place that monotonously drags on like a bad movie. Heaven is a place to look forward to and be expectant about, void of any sorrow and filled with complete joy! And Jesus is setting up a place for us because He knows one day we will arrive at our new home with a smile on our faces and joy in our hearts.

Heaven is your real home; it is eternal. Yet, don't be so focused on heaven that it distracts you from what God has for you right now. You were made to have an impact on this earth and then spend eternity in heaven. You have a place being prepared to reside when your body wears out and your race is over. Eternity with the Lord is not just a future benefit for you; it is your beautiful destination. Live for your purpose in the present knowing that you have a place prepared for you in paradise.

DAY 14
PRAY OFTEN

"Ask, and it will be given to you; seek, and you will find; knock, and it will be opened to you."
(Matthew 7:7)

Have you ever complained to God about something? You cannot complain to God about something if you've never prayed about it. You can hope really hard for something to happen or some problem to go away, but until you've prayed about it, nothing is going to change. You are not to give up before you seek God; you are not to get frustrated when your prayer isn't instantly answered. God wants you to seek Him avidly and often. Don't be afraid to pray to the Lord consistently for He loves to hear from you! You will never bother God with your many prayers!

Sometimes we have a desire on our heart, yet we do not take the time to pray about it. We might think about it a lot throughout the day, but we must remember that prayer is both active and interactive. Our thought life and our prayer life go hand in hand. As our mind is active, that is the time to let God know what's on your heart and what you are seriously thinking about. If I'm thinking of something and it's consuming me, my wife will know by the look on my face. So she'll ask me, "What are you thinking about?" I'll tell her and feel so much better because that one thought is off my chest and she'll be happy because I shared my heart with her. Similarly, the Lord knows what we think, and He wants us to share what's on our hearts with Him!

Prayer is a privilege! As we seek the Lord in prayer, we are communicating with the Creator of the universe, and He listens. That truth in itself is incredibly mind-blowing. The God who created and sustains the whole entire universe listens to each and every prayer that His children pray. Prayer is beyond powerful and it's when one prays that his vision becomes clear! When you ask, seek and knock, you are placing God as a first line of defense and a life priority. Communication with the Lord is and should be the number one focus each and every day of our lives! For the believer, prayer should not be a last resort. Many people view prayer as a last-ditch effort because nothing else they've tried worked. Prayer should be our first line of defense because it is incredibly powerful.

> Seeking God is the sure way to a clear path and an eternal perspective.

Prayer takes continual persistence and constant effort. Just because God did not answer your prayer the first time you communicated with Him does not mean you are to give up and pray for something else. We may give up on a few things in life because they aren't working out, but do not give up on prayer. In 1 Samuel, Hannah prayed passionately and persistently to have a baby. She did not give up, nor did she pray once and then get frustrated and go about her life totally defeated. Subsequently, God heard her cry and answered her fervent prayer. We have the opportunity to do the same thing with all that is on our hearts. We don't want to give up on prayer because we don't *feel* like God is listening to us. According to the Scriptures, we know that when we speak to God, His ears are attentive to our cries and pleas. Keep asking, seeking and knocking. If prayer were easy, I think most believers would actually pray a lot. The fact is that payer is laborious. It takes work; prayer is difficult. But it is a complete blessing and totally effective. God always comes through for those who pray. He hears, He cares.

If God has given you a clear-cut promise, keep on praying until that promise comes to pass. The Lord may tell you no, and that's fine because it's all about God's will and not your self-focused plans—the Lord's ways are completely perfect all the time. God's gentle voice leads our personal lives and guides our every step. Persistently praying means praying with a willing heart and open ears. Prayer isn't a monologue; it's a dialogue and we should listen to God as much as we talk to Him. Press into prayer for it is what makes life clear.

DAY 15
TRUE VALUE

Then Jesus looked around and said to His disciples, "How hard it is for those who have riches to enter the kingdom of God!" (Mark 10:23)

The love of money has thwarted the spiritual lives of many people. In the Scriptures, Jesus warns us about riches and the negative results if we let it take over our lives. Riches can blind the most committed Christ follower because money brings people a false sense of security.

You cannot serve both God and money. Maybe there have been moments in your life where you were living as if God was secondary. Things consumed you and caused your eyes to drift off of the Lord, pulling you away from the spiritual. What you place value on is what you will think about the most.

Before my family moved to the Deep South, we lived in Southern California. Out there so many people were OK with *not* following God because they had enough money and all that they need. It was sad actually because people measured other people, not by their character but by what and how much money and material items they owned. There was no room for God in their day-to-day lives! When a person lets money dominate and take control, they will not see God as a priority.

The problem is not with money itself; it can and should be used as a tool to live, provide, and glorify God. Money and riches become a problem when a person values it as the most important aspect of life! Money can be useful, helpful and enjoyable until it runs and rules a person at the expense of their relationship with God. When it comes to money, may we ask God for wisdom on how to use it and may we not let money consume us! We may not have a ton of extra money and we may not be rich, but still the love of money can cause our priorities to become way out of whack. Money can become a controlling "god" when it becomes everything to a person.

> When money is used as a tool to glorify God, it's a blessing; but when money becomes a god, it's consuming.

The more money we accumulate, the greater responsibility we have. Throughout my life as a believer, I've always had just enough money and not a huge surplus. I think God knows exactly how much I need to be responsible without spending carelessly or wasting the resources He's blessed me with. God has always provided for my family, and for that I am so grateful! We are not to waste our resources; we are to use them for a higher purpose. Money is an amazing tool given by God to expand His kingdom and make an eternal impact in this world. When we give with the motivation of pleasing God, we are using our money the way God intended it to be used. Our provision comes from our Provider and we don't *have to* give, we *get* to give. May we both enjoy what we are blessed with and use our blessings to bless others. We are so abundantly blessed by the Lord and not just materially. We have all the spiritual riches available in Christ Jesus—all that we have is from God! He is good all the time and we must keep our eyes on the Lord as He is and should be our first priority.

Remember to give God praise for all that He has provided for you. Don't let money rule, run and dictate your decisions in life and don't let money tear you away from the One who provides for you in the first place. A good thing can become a bad thing if it pulls us away from the only One who can fulfill. Enjoy the resources that you have and use what you are blessed with for the Lord. Every good and perfect gift comes from our good and perfect God (James 1:17).

DAY 16
HEARING GOD

"Heaven and earth will pass away, but My words will by no means pass away." (Luke 21:33)

When you get into God's Word, it will impact your life. As you read the pages of Scripture, you'll quickly realize that the Bible is *not* just a book with historical facts with cute little stories in it. God's Word is real, powerful and straight from the Lord to your very heart! The Bible is not just for other people, God's Word is for you! Know that as you delve into the Bible, the Lord will meet you right where you're at in life. The Bible is the only thing you will take to heaven with you. God's Word will exist forever. Long after we are gone, the Scriptures will still be working in power in the lives of believers.

People throughout history have tried to destroy God's Word from existence and balked at the thought of someone believing what they deem as myth and nonsense. Every attempt to eradicate the Bible has completely failed and will continue to fail. God's Word is old, but it is not, nor will it ever be, outdated. *Relevant* and *applicable* are a couple words that come to me as I think about God's love letter to us. How many times have we been reading or hearing Scriptures and the Lord meets us in our life circumstances? It happens to me all the time and it blows my mind!

When I was going to college at a super secular campus, I depended on the Word of God like never before. Almost everything the teachers taught and believed was the exact opposite of what the Bible says. In one of my classes on the first day, the professor asked the class, "Who in here is a born again Christian?" Come to find out throughout that semester, the professor's dad was a Christian and would try to share the Lord with him growing up. It made him so mad that his dad tried to convert him before he passed away, so the teacher hated those who were Christians. God uses His children as living Bibles and we get to share the truth with the world that is starving of something genuine and real! The Bible is not irrelevant or impersonal. God's Word is actually and emphatically living and active (Hebrews 4:12). God's Word can wreck us and then mend us. The Bible confronts us with conflict in our own hearts and then gives us the truth and tools to deal with those confrontations. The Word speaks to our situations and gives us truth and direction for our everyday lives. The Word is like good seed that is planted in our hearts and grows to such a point that it positively affects who we are. As we open God's Word, may it sink into our open hearts and continue to transform our lives!

> **The Bible is what God uses to meet us in our life circumstances.**

God's Word lives forever so that we can take it in and give it out. We soak in the Scriptures and let them speak to our life situations. Then we have the privilege to go out and share with others how God speaks through His Word! The Bible is not just a bound book that we open and learn from, or a book of nice moral stories that make us feel good. When opened, God's Word comes to reside within us, changing us from the inside out. Charles Spurgeon said, "Nobody ever outgrows scripture; the book widens and deepens with our years." We keep the Bible alive by sharing it with all who would hear! We pass on what has been passed on to us. As truth tellers in this world that is full of lies, it is such a blessing to take in God's Word and relay the reality of the gospel to this dying world. Let it have a mighty influence on your life and in the lives of those who surround you. God's Word is alive and we get to share it while we are living. Thank You, God!

Please remember that God's words to your life will give you such clarity for your God-given journey. The Scriptures will always speak to you as you stay in them consistently and daily. Keep your heart open, your ears attentive and your life impressionable to what the Lord wants to say to you presently. His living Word will speak to your life on a constant basis. You will pass away one day and be in the presence of the Lord. Even then, God's words will continue on. His Word is everlasting. Take God's Word to heart, hear Him speak and watch Him work!

DAY 17

SUFFERING

"For I will show him how many things he must suffer for My name's sake." (Acts 9:16)

What you go through in this life has a purpose behind it. You've been through your share of difficulties and it may have been unclear what the purpose of those difficulties were. Please remember that God can use every single conflict that you face for the good! God does not waste any trial that you go through. He can use your toughest time as a testimony to others. To suffer for the Lord is actually a noble action because it demonstrates that you are actively living for the Lord.

To suffer means to be in some kind of distress or hardship. In America we may not be put to death for being Jesus believers, but we do face pushback in other ways. As we live out our faith, people may criticize, mock and ridicule us. Even though we are a Christian nation, still some people hate church, the Bible, and God. Pushback can result in personal distress, deep depression and a lowered countenance. It doesn't feel good when we face ridicule for living in accordance with what the Bible says.

The fact is that I used to be one of those who ridiculed the faith and mocked people who went to church. Not because I hated the people practicing their faith, I just didn't understand the truth! If you are facing difficulties for being bold in the faith, take heart! Don't give in to any negative results from following Jesus but instead know that it's a sign that you are living for the Lord. I've been laughed at for being a Christian, but to tell you the truth, I don't care. I'd rather be laughed at on this earth and spend eternity with the Lord than be liked on this earth and spend eternity separated from Jesus. Know that not everyone will agree with the truth. Many will fight against what you believe and may think you are foolish for having faith. We are not called to be comfortable; we are called to be content in every situation. In certain situations we may suffer for our Savior, but that's nothing compared to what He's gone through for us.

> Continue to love those who totally disagree with you, for your attitude can be a beacon of light for the faith you're living out.

We may make some people angry when we talk about our faith and share the gospel. People may have animosity toward us as Christians because we believe the Bible passionately. But our response to these negative reactions should be to continue to love and pray for those who are against what God says. Jesus never said we are to condemn our enemies, nor let them make us completely bitter and discouraged. Before Saul got saved and his name was changed to Paul, he hated Christians and persecuted them like crazy! Then the Lord Jesus met him on the Damascus road and his life was changed. He had to go through some seriously uncomfortable circumstances as God was transforming His mind and renewing his heart. He went from being the person persecuting to the person who was persecuted. Think about how radical it would be to actually encourage your adversaries and be kind to the who wanted to kill you! That was Paul. That should be us as well. Stand firm on Christ, your solid foundation. Embrace whatever uncomfortable situations or distressing circumstances you face. In the Sermon on the Mount, Jesus said that those who suffer persecution are blessed because they live for the Lord.

Being uncomfortable for God is a good thing. When you step out in faith, sometimes it is messy and full of drama. It usually isn't a smooth transition devoid of difficulties and integrated with situational perfection. Sometimes the result from boldly following Jesus is conflict and distress, pushback and mockery. Sometimes you will suffer for your Savior in ways you never thought you would. Yet, do *not* be discouraged. Take heart and have faith that God has you and will give you all the strength and wisdom you need to get through those situations you will face. Every time you step out in faith, God equips you with courage to share and a heart to love. It's time to step out.

DAY 18
FEAR AND FAITH

> *As soon as Jesus heard the word that was spoken, He said to the ruler of the synagogue, "Do not be afraid; only believe."* (Mark 5:36)

Allow faith to crowd out fear in your life. As the Lord Jesus speaks to you, listen to Him for He will graciously give you the assurance and the peace you need in and through your life. True peace, rest and relief doesn't come from a situation, it comes from your Savior! Look to Him first and know that He is not off in the distance at some far away location; He is close, He is near, He is with you.

Fear and faith are fierce enemies. They cannot live together. If we are fearful, then faith will be washed away and if we have faith, then fear is crowded out. Speaking to the ruler of the synagogue, Jesus made it clear what this fearful man needed to focus on. He needed to focus on faith in the Lord so his fear would dissipate. Before I was a Christian I would worry about so many things. I would think of all the what ifs, and these hypothetical situations would freak me out! When God rescued me and I began walking with Him, my fears began to vanish and I quickly realized that when I focused on the Lord, I did not need to fear! When Jesus is the center of our affection, then faith will result. We don't have faith in faith; we are to have faith in Jesus knowing that

He goes before us and paves a way where we see no way. As Christians we must put forward momentum to our faith. We must live by faith and walk by faith. We must never forget that the object of our faith is Jesus. The more consistently we look to Him, the clearer our vision will become. As we lean upon the Lord with our whole life, fear will not have a place to reside in our minds and hearts.

> **Fear is a byproduct of broken cohesion with God but faith is a byproduct of connection with Jesus.**

The enemy loves when our faith is passive and inactive. He loves when we allow fear to take over the forefront of our minds and daily pervade our lives. Because the devil hates us, he loves to see us anxious, stressed and fearful. Therefore, he will use any tactic to deter us from depending on the Lord. If he can keep us in fear, then faith will be kept at a distance. If he can make us uneasy with what God has called us to, then anxiety will be the norm in our lives and inactivity will result. We have to remember that we are in a battle that has already been won. The enemy is defeated, yet he keeps fighting. As long as we are alive and breathing, the devil will be opposing anything we do in the name of the Lord. The way to let fear fall is to focus on Jesus and know that He gives us boldness and courage to fight this battle of faith. Corrie Ten Boom said, "Faith is like radar that sees through the fog—the reality of things at a distance that the human eye cannot see." There truly is an unseen spiritual battle going on but as we live by faith, we will have total assurance that the Lord has and will have the victory!

You can know with confidence that Christ is with you and therefore, you have nothing to fear. When Jesus is the center of your affections, the enemy's distractions fade into the distance. Continue to pray for your faith to flourish because a growing faith is an unstoppable faith. Keep progressing in the promises of God and don't back down from what the Lord has called you to do. To simply believe sounds easy, but it takes a consistent and concerted effort to daily focus on Jesus. Do not allow your life to be run and dictated by feelings, let it be run by faith in your limitless and unstoppable God! You will never regret it.

DAY 19

REACH OUT

> *"Heal the sick, cleanse the lepers, raise the dead, cast out demons. Freely you have received, freely give."* (Matthew 10:8)

God wants to use you in mighty ways! It is a total blessing to serve God by reaching out to others. You are not called to be a perpetual taker; you are called to give—give out what God has given you. Every believer, including you, is a minister of the gospel. This means you have the great privilege to get up and get out into the world to share the truth with lost and dying souls. You get to serve God by reflecting Him to people who need to be saved. How amazing is that!

Doing ministry is not for the faint of heart; it's hard work! As believers, we are all called to connect with people and share the gospel. I think sometimes we forget that we must all play a large part in the body of Christ! Christian workers, pastors and worship leaders are not the only ones called to the ministry. Every believer is called to step up and reach out to broken people and let them know God can heal and mend them. It may seem like a burden at times to get out of our comfort zone for the sake of a soul, but it's what we are called to do. Often I'm reminded how just *one* soul is so important to God. Having a heart for the lost is the heart that the Lord wants us to have. I am so thankful for those people who shared the gospel with me! They were bold and unashamed to share the message that totally transformed my heart and mind (Romans 1:16). Now that I'm walking with the Lord, it's time for me to grab the baton and share with those who are lost and living in their sin. It's not a burden to reach out to people who are in desperate need of hope, it's a blessing! And to see someone come to Christ and find comfort in Christ is so rewarding it really will fire us up!

We cannot mend people back together, but we can share the gospel and watch as the Lord makes them whole. As we reach out, the Lord meets individuals in their time of need. God desires to use you to share His message that will rescue lost people out of the quicksand of the world. We get to be used as vessels to help others know that in Jesus, there is victory.

> Grab the hand of the lost and with God's strength, pull them out of the darkness of sin.

We are blessed in so many ways in this life as we are the recipients of God's gifts. God has given us so much in the way of spiritual blessings and even material blessings. We don't deserve what we've been blessed with but that doesn't stop God from overwhelming us with every good gift! Yet, with the gifts that we are given, it is our duty and privilege to look outside of ourselves and meet the need of others. When we only focus on ourselves, we will be the most miserable people in the world. When we look beyond ourselves and seek out the hurting and hungry crowds, that will be the start of selfless living. May we bring the comfort of the Lord to those who are helpless and hurting. May we act on every God-given opportunity to be there for someone, to come alongside them, and share God's heart with them and let them know there is a God who absolutely loves them! What a blessed privilege we have to do ministry by simply reaching out where God has presently placed us.

Daily you have opportunity to pour yourself out for people. Ministry happens when you are a light in your day-to-day life by seeing the needs of others and letting people know God will fulfill those needs. You can have a huge impact to those around you by stepping out and reaching out with uninhibited boldness. Pray that God would lead and guide as you minister to others.

DAY 20
HAVE COMPASSION

"I have compassion on the multitude, because they have now continued with Me three days and have nothing to eat." (Mark 8:2)

God always has compassion for you. He sees your needs and He is with you through every single mountaintop moment and through every deep dark valley. He cares about the challenges you face and will provide for you in ways that you may not see right now. Jesus will not walk by you and keep going —His presence is with you every step of the way. Believe it!

His compassion led Jesus to take action toward people who were hungry and needy. *Compassion* means "to have a desire to relieve suffering." Jesus saw the hunger of the people and did something about it rather than ignore the need or see them as a nuisance. At times we see a need and hope someone else takes care of it because it may be uncomfortable or inconvenient to help. Yet, if God calls us to step up and reach out to someone who is down and out, then we must step up and take that God-given opportunity. There may be no one else to help that hurting person who is right in front of you. If the Holy Spirit prompts us to take action when we see a need, then it should be our pleasure to be led by the Spirit to fulfill that call.

There have been numerous times over the years where the Holy Spirit called me to do something or talk to someone and I flat out refused! I look back at those moments and cringe because I was thinking of myself rather than the other person! We've all missed divine opportunities from the Lord because we have been so inwardly focused. We need to look up and walk forward in what the Holy Spirit is leading us to do! Now is not the time to sit on the sidelines and remain dormant for our God. This dark world is not going to get any brighter by just hoping someone else helps out. May we be boots on the ground believers every day of our lives! It's time to not just watch the game but to get into the game and win people to Christ!

> **Now is the time to let the Holy Spirit lead your every step.**

We were created out of the Father's love; the Lord sees us as His poem, His song and His work of art. We may not always feel loved, but the fact is that God's love is forever for us. He cares that people suffer in this sinful and fallen world and He wants to use you and me to relay the reality of the gospel to them. God wants us to be there for those who are struggling, hurting and in pain. It is true that without the Lord we cannot offer any lasting assistance and absolutely no eternally-based help. As we reach out to the downtrodden and hungry, may we share the Lord with them, for He offers everlasting help that every human being needs. God's assistance never disappoints; it leads to healing, mending and clarity and fulfills that spiritual hunger inside of every human being.

It is a privilege to be used by God to fulfill a need. Make sure you have your eyes open to see the need of those truly suffering. God puts people in your life so that you would see them and have compassion upon them. He places those who are desperate in front of you, not so you can fix them yourself or be their functional savior; but so that you can direct their eyes to the very heart of God. May you have the compassion of your Creator to meet those desperate needs around you. May the love of the Lord be shared from your mouth to those hurting hearts you interact with. Don't be afraid but ask the Lord for serious boldness and heavenly bravery and He will give it to you. When your eyes are on Jesus, your eyes are open to those who need Him.

DAY 21
HEED GOD

"Remember Lot's wife." (Luke 17:32)

Don't look back to who you used to be or to what you used to do. You can't control what has already happened. The past is over and you need to let go of those things that have already occurred. God has worked on your heart and you are not the same person you once were. You are stronger now. God has given you a new heart and you've been freed from the power of habitual sin. Know God is presently working on your heart and He will continue to as you move forward in the faith.

The word Jesus used for *remember* means "to learn a lesson from." The angel specifically told Lot and his family not to "lag behind." So Lot's wife disobeyed a specific word from the Lord. When we remember Lot's wife, it teaches us a lesson about the danger of not listening to the Lord. If you have kids, you know how it affects you when your children are *not* listening when you are attempting to get through to them. So you set consequences for their disobedience. Or maybe in your job there are times where employees decide not to listen to the boss or directly go against his plans. That boss will not just brush off their disobedience, there will be write ups or even terminations!

The fact is that we are not called to obey the Lord when it's convenient or when we feel like it. We are not called to follow God once in a while or only on Sundays. We are called to obey the Lord every day and all the time because He always knows best! God is the only know-it-all in the universe, and that's a good thing! As our ears are attentive and our hearts are willing to hear God's voice, we will run our race unhindered. Disobedience toward God never turns out well for us and nothing good ever results. Simply put, God's Word teaches us what to do and what not to do. If God tells you not to look back and instead to focus forward, then don't look back—focus forward. I'm not trying to be facetious or flippant I'm just stating the fact that obeying the Lord is what this life is about. May we continue on with the Lord, following Him, listening to Him and aligning our hearts to His.

> When God's ways are heeded, then we can know we are on the road of His will.

If we are gazing back where we came from, we will not get to where we're going. God has a divine plan for us, and it will come to fruition under one condition: our obedience. Lot's wife did not listen to the Lord's leading and therefore, she was stopped dead in her tracks. Life is short and there is no time to be idle or meander around, attempting to execute our own plans and doing our own thing. God created a purpose and plan for our lives. Our part is to grow toward God and fulfill His will. Forward momentum for God's kingdom happens as our eyes stay focused on our eternal God.

We learn from what happened with Lot's wife that hesitating to heed God's Word is never good. The times that I hesitated when God said go forward have resulted in some very difficult seasons in my life. Often the result is heartache and even divine consequences when we can sometimes be stubborn toward what God wants. Sorry but you're not the exception. We are all human and we can all be stubborn at times. At the end of the day, the Lord knows what's best and we don't. The fact is that a surrendered heart leads to God's desired destination for us.

It's time to make it a continual habit to hear and heed the Lord. He knows what's best for your daily life so don't backtrack in your walk with Him. Don't go back to what God has already called you out of. Don't hesitate when the Lord tells you to get up and get going or to stay put and wait on Him. He doesn't lead you to take action because He's mean and wants you to be miserable. He calls you to take action because His will for your life is the road that leads to joy, fulfillment and a heightened countenance. The Lord has brought you out of the miry clay called the world and has set you upon the Rock. Stay founded upon that Rock and don't look back. Continue to plow ahead, allowing God to fully lead your life. You will never regret it!

DAY 22
BE AWARE

"And Jesus answered and said to them: 'Take heed that no one deceives you.'" (Matthew 24:4)

The devil hates you. He wants nothing more than for you to believe his lies and buy into unfounded doubt and discouragement. He wants you to abandon the faith and believe that the world and its evil ways are where real life is at. Don't let him deceive you and don't let his outlandish lies sway you away from the Lord. Instead, stand strong in the Lord and in the power of His might. Follow God and feed off of His wisdom and never stop going forward in the faith. God will give you all you need to walk in truth so that no lie can blindside you.

If deceit shows up at your doorstep, turn the lights out and don't answer. The Lord knocks on the door of our heart, but the devil tries to get into our head. How many times have we bought into the discouraging thoughts that the enemy hurls at us? Every time I allow discouraging thoughts to fester in my mind, it brings me down and fills me with despair. Those thoughts don't come from God; they always come from the devil. Even as believers, the devil can bring oppression into our life and doubt to our mind.

I remember there was a new believer who was just learning the foundations of the faith. She prayed that even Satan would be saved! Although this was a prayer from a sincere heart, theologically it is an impossibility. The devil is an enemy that we are not called to love and who will never be saved. Pretty crazy to think about that fact. As the enemy whispers lies to you, reject those lies right away and walk away from him. Pray that God would protect your mind and extract thoughts that are clearly not of God. Satan may attempt to bring deceivers into your life to share half-truths which could be very dangerous. We have the whole truth and as we stay in it consistently, we will be able to quickly spot a lie and reject it. We can fight deceit by getting into God's Word to get complete clarity.

> We are called to resist the devil and rest in the Lord.

When we are weak, we are susceptible to deceit. It's in those dark places when we are alone that God's still small voice can get drowned out by the devil's obnoxious enticements. This is why we desperately need the truth of God's Word to give us strength. The truth is the measuring rod that we constantly live in and look toward. If something does not line up with the truth, we must quickly throw it out. Many people give in to deceit when they are down, discouraged, or depressed. But those are the moments when we need to desperately begin clinging to the Lord. The devil will bring deceivers in the very midst of our distress in an attempt to blur the line between good and evil. Do not give in! May we be so filled with the Word of God that there is no room for any lies to reside in our minds. Be aware of the enemy's tactics and beware of those who nonchalantly attempt to cause you to question what you know is true!

Continue consistently in God's Word so as to recognize and reject the horrible lies from below. Deceit that sometimes seeps into your mind will be destroyed as you constantly depend upon God, yielding to Him completely. As you surrender to the Lord of hosts, you'll see clearly that it's God who is fighting for you. You will be given complete clarity as you hear from your Creator through prayer and His amazing Word. The Bible, coupled with the power of the Holy Spirit, will give you discernment to spot and deflect deceit and walk joyously in the truth. Continue to walk by faith and as you do, God will reveal to you what is true and what is not.

DAY 23

SURRENDERED

Jesus said to him, "You shall love the LORD your God with all your heart, with all your soul, and with all your mind." (Matthew 22:37)

The Bible is clear—either you give Him all or you give Him nothing at all. He is an all-or-nothing God! It is time to quit holding back and start moving forward in total surrender to the One who gave you life. You can't afford to be a half-hearted Christian. There's no time to be sitting on the fence contemplating whether you should fully follow God or not. Time is short and therefore, it is time to focus on the priorities of life. Raise your hands, your heart, and your life to God because the time was not yesterday, the time is now!

In today's Scripture, Jesus is reiterating the Shema from Deuteronomy 6:4-9. It's important for the believer to read these passages and be reminded that surrender is not an option, it is a necessity. When in battle and the enemy has you cornered, that's the time to raise your hands in defeat. Yet, surrendering to God is both the same and different. What I mean is that when we surrender to God, we do raise our hands, not in defeat but in dependence. Yes, we give up our lives and yield to God in submission but that doesn't mean we are victims or losers. Surrendering to God means loving God, putting Him first, and letting nothing creep up on our hearts ahead of Him.

There are things in this world that vie for our attention and many of those things are very unhealthy. We can tend to give our time and energy to actions and hobbies that make no difference in this life; they end up being a waste of time. I don't want to waste the short amount of time I have on this earth focusing on stuff that doesn't even matter! Instead, I want to surrender to the Lord and seek Him with all that I am, don't you? To pursue God is to navigate in the direction of the Lord every single day which is such an amazing privilege. Jesus should be the top priority of our lives! Worship the Lord with all of what He has made you and give every ounce of your affection to the Lord. Today is the day to place both feet into the purpose of furthering eternity. He doesn't want weekend visitors or believers who carve out time to come to church on a couple holidays through the years. He wants non-stop connection with you. It's time to love the Lord fully and go all in for Him.

> Surrender isn't a state of mind. It is a daily action you are called to take in regard to your Christian life.

The heart is the core of the Christian being and the core of all that we are. When we are willing to give in to who God is, the result is total submission. This is the best action we could ever take! Jesus is saying that as we yield to God, we are denying self-absorption and embracing self-denial. It's so easy to focus on self for our society celebrates selfishness and balks at selflessness. In reality though, who cares what society thinks? This world is not our destination, nor are we living to make a permanent home on this earth. We are here for a short while and then we die. While we are camping on this earth, we'd do well to hear God, heed Him, and walk in the direction He is guiding us in.

The question may come up, "Why should we follow the Lord and what makes you think His way is the best way?" Obedience and submission toward the Lord are desirable because of His beautiful attributes. He is loving, kind, gracious and merciful. God wants the best for us and we are most blessed when we are walking in the center of His will. When we halfheartedly live for Him and practice partial obedience, we suffer and become miserable. Selfishness is innate because we were born into sin. Selflessness is simply raising our hands and reverting our eyes to the Lord.

Love the Lord with your whole life and surrender to Him your all. When you do, watch how greatly God can use you as you love Him above everything else in this bleak world. Now is the time to go forward with the Lord and position yourself in the center of the mission He has for you. Then God will be able to use you mightily and to capacity. When you surrender to God, you will never be the same.

DAY 24
GOD'S WILL

And He said, "Abba, Father, all things are possible for You. Take this cup away from Me; nevertheless, not what I will, but what You will." (Mark 14:36)

When you are walking in God's will, you will find yourself where God wants you to be. You were made to live in the middle of the mission and purpose that God has for you. As you seek God for direction and guidance into His perfect plan, He will answer you and direct your steps. There are times where it may not be easy for you to live out the will of God, yet it will be worth it.

God is more than able to do what we might label as impossible. The Lord's ways are way better and much higher than our ways for He knows exactly what He is doing. God completely shatters our limited view and He wrecks the thought of actual impossibilities. Do you believe the Lord can do anything? Are you convinced that God can work miraculously and turn the toughest situations around? Have faith that God can, and don't doubt His power and sovereignty.

Those moments in my life where things seemed chaotic, I would remind myself that God has me, is with me and in complete control. It doesn't matter how I feel, nor does it matter that my situation looked hopeless. God can take a chaotic mess and birth an amazing miracle out of it. Sometimes we categorize what we think God can and can't do based on what we see with our eyes. One of the amazing things about the Lord is that He sees what we can't see, and all things are possible for Him. The Lord's plans and purposes should matter to us more than anything in this life. Jesus was struggling in the garden, seeking God to make sure that suffering on the cross was in God's divine plans. Jesus took on the wrath of God on our behalf and became a curse so we could be forgiven. This action was obviously no small feat and yet Jesus had confirmation from the Lord and went through what He went through for you and me.

> Impossibilities need to be extracted from our vocabulary because from God's view there are no impossibilities.

Jesus gave us an example of how to continually connect to the Father in order to follow and honor Him. Our connection with our Creator is the most important relationship in this life; it is the relationship that we should foster the most! Therefore, we must intentionally spend time seeking God, talking to Him and pouring out our hearts to Him. Praying to the Lord is not always easy and is often a struggle. But at the end of the day God has all the answers we need.

The times where I struggled with accepting God's will and I rejected what He wanted me to do, I thought it'd be easier to just do what I thought was right and disregard everything else. Every single time I had this mindset and I did my own thing, I ended up striving more than ever! When I totally surrendered to God's will, even when it was difficult, then I was able to actually have a settled heart and a purpose-driven perspective. God's will may not look easy on the outset but as we accept it and walk in it, we realize it is the right thing to do and the right way to go.

Stay closely connected to your Father through prayer. The Creator of the universe wants to hear from you. As you are totally honest about your struggles, He wants you to seek Him and make sure you are in the middle of His purpose and on the road of His will. Be obedient to Him and the outcome will align with God's perfect and impeccable will. God longs to impart His will to your very life on a daily basis. He knows what you face and even when His will seems hard, He will give you the strength, wisdom, endurance and perseverance you need to accomplish your heavenly calling. All that is required from you is that you listen and stay consistent in seeking Him.

DAY 25
RESIST

> *Then Jesus said to him, "Away with you, Satan! For it is written, You shall worship the LORD your God, and Him only you shall serve."*
> (Matthew 4:10)

The lure of the enemy can be incredibly strong and constant. The enemy will never stop tempting you, but God will never stop fighting for you. It is the enemy's goal to take you down and stop your spiritual progress. He works overtime and will stop at nothing to take you away from fellowship and the Word of God. As you are tempted, remember that the Word of God has the power to help you resist temptation and stand firm in the faith. Make it a habit to use God's Word as a weapon to fight against the enemy's tactics. It works!

We must intentionally seek God so as to fight against the one who wants to steal, kill and destroy. Testing often follows triumphs. We see this incredible scene in the gospels where the Father speaks, the Holy Spirit descends, and Jesus gets baptized. You'd think after this powerful moment that Jesus would go straight to the ministry and do radical, amazing and powerful work. Instead, He is led to the desert where He fasts, and at His weakest point the devil temps Him like crazy!

Some of the most powerful moments in my walk with the Lord were followed by some of my deepest trials. Over the last decade and a half, my wife and I have had the privilege to do ministry together and see God do amazing feats. One thing we do regularly, especially when we are about to do something big for God, is we pray together. We seek God for cohesion and protection because we know that now that we are stepping out in faith, we will face opposition on a large scale. The devil hates us and wants to discourage and deflate our very countenance. On the other hand, the Lord wants to shine His light into our lives, lift us up, and encourage us. We can fight temptation by immersing in the living Word of God. And remember that we worship only One! Satan is not the opposite of God; he is a created being and he will be defeated and God will be victorious!

> The way to resist the enemy's opposition is to seek God and turn the battle over to Him.

Giving glory to God should be our motivation in all that we do in this life. He is and should be the center of our service! Every day we have the opportunity to do all that we do unto the Lord. This means we work for Him, live to please Him and worship Him alone. Satan attempts to steal our allegiance and I hate to say it, but his tactics are working. So many people these days are walking away from the Lord, from church and from truth, and it grieves God so much. The Bible alludes to this sad fact as people who were once on fire for the Lord "exchange the truth of God for a lie" (Romans 1:25). I've personally known a handful of people who were inspirational in my life because they had such strong faith; yet they let the world, the devil and the flesh get the best of them and they ended up forsaking the truth, allowing lies into their lives. Now they are lost, confused and walking in darkness.

It's important to remember that the evil one cannot possess the believer, but he can oppress and plant evil thoughts inside our heads. Ultimately though, he has no power to overtake the Lord's people as long as we are surrendered to Him. So many are straying from the faith because they are not fully invested and committed to Jesus. James tells us to resist the devil—and he is completely right! The Lord has given us all the spiritual weapons we need to fight against the enemy and allow God to defeat him on a daily basis. There will be temptations and trials but don't forget that the Lord is stronger than any circumstances you face.

The battle is not easy but God has given you the tools and the spiritual arsenal to fight the enemy. Put the armor on, memorize Scriptures and know that God has your back. He is interceding for you and fighting for you every single day and He'll never stop. It's up to you to stick close to God and to be on guard, using the resources God has blessed you with. May you be Father-focused on a daily basis for the Lord is your helper, healer and provider. Make Him the center of your affections and know that temptations can always be resisted because God is fighting for you.

DAY 26
GOD'S HOUSE

> *Then He taught, saying to them, "Is it not written, 'My house shall be called a house of prayer for all nations?' But you have made it a den of thieves."* (Mark 11:17)

God's house should be the safest place to be, where we can rest and get rejuvenated in the Word of God! The church is not man-made, rather it is designed and set up by the Lord Himself. The book of Acts is a blueprint of what church activities must consist of. It is a wake-up call to the reality that we all need to be plugged into a body of believers on a regular basis. We were designed to fellowship; we were not meant to live this life alone to try and figure life out separated from other believers.

The church is the place you and I can plug in and connect with other people who absolutely love the Lord! As we gather with other believers, we'll have people to pray with, intercede for and lift up, and worship the Lord with. God's house is most alive and thriving when the early church activities as seen in Acts 2:42 are the main occurrence. It is where we spiritually grow, be refreshed and encouraged!

The building that we meet in is *not* the church, *we* are the church! Nonetheless, the facility where we meet should be set apart for the Lord, dedicated for His use, and built upon the Lord. When the church building is anything other than spiritual, it becomes so superficial and spiritually unhealthy. The things of the world should not seep into the church and influence it with its trends and popular activities. When I walk into a church building and it's just like a club, I will not stay because I know I will not learn or grow in my faith there. I don't go to church for entertainment and I don't form my opinion of a church based on the worship team or the pastor's "performance." I don't care about all that. I could care less if the pastor is boring or enthusiastic or if the lights are cool looking or if there is a fog machine. What I care about, and I think what we all should care about, is the content of the worship songs that are being sung and Word that is being preached! Is it biblically sound and in context, or is it springboard teaching where one verse is read and then everything else is out of context? The church should definitely be all about love but it should also always be all about the truth. We gather together to seek God and hear His voice. We meet not to have some surface level social club interaction; we meet to see our lives built up in the faith and get refocused on what matters in this life.

The church is *not* perfect because it's made up of imperfect people. The church is God's people who are looking to the Lord and leaning toward the Lord. We are all being refined as we gather together and practice the four church activities in Acts 2:42 on a regular basis. It has been rightly said that the church should be where God's people come in broken and bruised and leave healed and encouraged. When

Jesus is the foundation that the church is built upon, it will thrive, bear fruit and become training ground for encouragement.

> We gather together to get encouraged in content rather than entertainment.

Scandal, slander, deceit and drama have no place in the house of God. We're not called to slander people with a smile or to compare ourselves with other "less spiritual people." The church doesn't exist in order to form an *us versus them* dichotomy. We don't gather together to form a tribe and act like our tribe is the best in the city. We don't gather together to form cliques or clubs that excludes a bunch of other people in the church. We gather together for the purpose of worshiping the Lord, focusing on Him and growing in the faith!

Jesus made the purpose of church clear—it is to be a house of prayer. If you attend a church and there is as much drama in that place as in the world, I'd recommend leaving. God has an amazing way of removing those people that cause conflict and drama from the church. I've seen it time and time again and it gives me such confidence in the Lord that He will protect and defend His church. We go to a gathering of believers to gain strength from God in a safe place that preaches truth in love and lets God be the Judge. We should be able to let down our guard and be somewhat vulnerable in a church setting. A healthy church is one that focuses on Jesus and reveres God, instead of being flippant about Jesus and not taking God seriously.

Make it a godly habit to attend a church you can call home. The gathering place where you attend should be a safe place to allow the Lord to rejuvenate and strengthen you. If you change churches often, then it may not be the church that needs to change, it may be your heart that needs to change. Instead of attending a church based on what *you* can get out of it, attend a church with the mindset of *how can I serve in this place?* It will make all the difference. God's house should have an atmosphere where you can be vulnerable, where it's safe to cry out to the Lord—to be honest before Him, to pray unashamed, to seek Him with your whole heart. The world beats you up, but the church must build you up.

DAY 27
RESCUED

"I have come as a light into the world, that whoever believes in Me should not abide in darkness." (John 12:46)

Jesus is the light of the world and He has caught your attention so much so that you've started following Him and doing what He wants you to do. He's pulled you out of darkness and now real life is illuminated as you live to further the kingdom of God. As you navigate through this fallen world, remember that the darkness has dissipated and the light of Jesus continually shines. Part of your testimony is that you were saved because light has come into the world. How amazing is that!

I wasn't even aware how dark my life was until the Lord Jesus grabbed my attention and caused me to question the way I was living and what I was living for. Jesus turned on a light in my heart and lit up those dark corners of sin in my life so that I could come clean and turn away from evil! Jesus is the light of the world and He is the gift that arrived to conquer death and defeat the enemies that threaten us. If we peer into this place we call the world for any length of time, we realize that it continues to grow darker and darker. The news that we hear is most often bad as the majority of people in the world love the darkness, not realizing they are miserable. They are stuck and their world is dim. They don't want to escape the darkness because they are too in love with their wicked ways. They need the eternal light to spiritually see on this temporal earth. Jesus came into the world to rescue us from the dark, restore broken souls, and open our eyes to see.

I ran from the light on a regular basis until there came a point where weariness and emptiness collided. I was hopeless and lost thinking life was purposeless. When I stopped running and started seeking, I realized the Lord had always been there calling me to Himself. What I quickly realized when I began my walk with the Lord was that Jesus came into the world to bring light to my life and set me free.

> **Jesus came into this world to light up the hearts of those who live in the dark.**

When we believe in Jesus, we become free in this life. We no longer abide or live in the darkness but the light of the of the Lord illuminates our understanding and flows out of us reflecting Jesus to others. There are so many people who abide in darkness and feel trapped and stuck in their sin without realizing there is an escape route. Jesus is the door that sinners open to get out of that house which lacks light! *Abide* actually means "to live in" or "to make one's home in." The truth is that there is still hope even for those who have made their dwelling place in the dark. Jesus made it clear that we live in the world, but we are not of the world. So as we live for Him, may we have a sense of urgency when it comes to lost souls and share with them our rescue story. We've been given the light so we can navigate through this waiting room called the world.

Please know that Jesus was born, died and rose again to dig you out of the darkness. You are saved and set apart for Him. Jesus, the greatest gift given to humanity, arrived on this earth to rescue you from the darkness and your self-destructive path. The road of God's will is lit up with His Word and with Jesus so you can see where God is leading you. You once were abiding in darkness but now you are living in the light. You are a sojourner who is here for a short time, whose divine path is illuminated by the Lord. Continue to live in the light and shine His light to a darkened world!

DAY 28

PRAYING WITH FAITH

"And whatever things you ask in prayer, believing, you will receive." (Matthew 21:22)

If you pray without believing that God will answer, then you are praying in vain. As you seek the Lord, make sure that you pray in faith knowing that God will come through. Seek the Lord with a heart that does not doubt and dedicated to seeing and anticipating an answer. As you pray, the Holy Spirit directs your prayer, and it is amazing!

Prayer without faith is futile. We can pray all day to the Lord, but if we are not believing He will answer, we are wasting our time. It's like someone talking for a long time and yet not really saying anything, like a politician doing a filibuster. It is a blessing that the Lord wants us to come to Him openly and honestly. It's not a bad thing to come to the Lord with our frustration and doubt. Even for those who have a hard time with heart sharing, we can and should completely share our hearts with God. But as we pray, I think it's a good practice to realize and remember who God is and what He can do. Impossibilities don't exist with God; He can do anything.

There have been numerous times where I sought the Lord more out of routine than with a heart of faith. At other times I would be seeking the Lord and my mind totally wandered and I forgot what I was supposed to pray for. It's like reading a book, and after a chapter or two, I realize I don't have a clue what I've just read. And I believe most of us can relate to this, especially when we attempt to pray at night in bed and then begin to snooze. Prayer is labor intensive, and I believe it's supposed to be. British Christian Missionary William Carey said, "Prayer—secret, fervent, believing prayer—lies at the root of all personal godliness." Believing is synonymous with faith. God can answer your prayer in an instant, or God may give you peace as you wait. We may want a yes to our prayer, but the Lord may say no. The bottom line is the Lord knows best! So as we pray in faith believing He will answer, His answer may be different than what we want, and that is a good thing! We may struggle in prayer, but God will soothe our heart and direct our lives as we pray.

Without faith our prayers are hollow.

If we don't communicate with God, then our relationship with Him will not be fostered. My wife and I were married June 24, 2006. I can honestly say after all these years, I know her better now than I've ever known her. We grow closer with every passing year because we spend time together, talk to one another and share our hearts. Similarly, we are to take these same actions in our relationship with the Lord! We need to seek Him and share our heart with God. But don't just speak to Him, create space to listen to what He wants to say in response to our believing faith-filled prayer.

There are moments where we become timid and we hold back in life. When it comes to prayer, let your inhibitions fall to the ground and just be honest with your God. Prayer is the least practiced activity among Christians but the most important action to take. With prayer comes power. We should desire nothing more than to communicate with our Creator who avidly wants to hear from us. To be active in prayer is to be honed in to our God. Praying to the Lord actually gives us the answer to our purpose in this life. It may seem extremely obvious but sometimes we forget that answers don't come if we don't ask. Answers come as we consistently, actively and honestly seek the Lord.

Have faith as you fall on your face before the Lord. Believe that God already knows every struggle you encounter, every storm you face and every pain you're experiencing. Have a heart that is in constant contact with the Lord and don't let the enemy come in and bring discouragement and doubt to your mind. Pray with faith, knowing your God will hear your pleas and give you clear direction for your life! Don't be afraid to pray big, honest and life-altering prayers. The bottom line is to pray on a consistent basis because it's your privilege and God wants to hear from you and have a dialogue rather than a monologue. Pray with faith—God is listening.

DAY 29

KINGDOM BUSINESS

But Jesus answered them, "My Father has been working until now, and I have been working."
(John 5:17)

You were created to work for the Lord and serve Him with your whole life. It is never a burden for you to get up and get actively going in the name of Lord. As you live your life, remember to do everything as unto the Lord and not because you want to be seen (Colossians 3:23). Glory belongs to God, not you. Jesus is our example and since He worked incredibly hard for His Father in heaven and everything He did was to point people's hearts to God, you and I are called to do the same.

Works has become sort of a bad word in the Christian world. Some groups of believers stay away from the word *works* because we all know a person isn't saved by their works. And so they are a bit afraid of even using that word when talking about their faith. Yes, we are saved by grace through faith (Ephesians 2:8-9), but then we begin living for the Lord and serving God! One phrase that helps me remember that I am to be an active kingdom participant is we are saved and then set to work. I'll never forget when I was a manager doing group interviews for a retail job. This one teenager was slouched down in a chair and looking like he did *not* really want to be at this interview. I asked him, "Why do you want this job?"

He answered and said, "Because I need the money." Yeah, I didn't hire him. It seemed like the interview and this job was going to be a burden for him and he was only in it for the money and not for the life experience.

We have the privilege to work for the Lord and be about His business, just like Jesus was even before He was a teenager (Luke 2:49). To be spent spiritually is actually very fulfilling because we're working directly for God! We have the opportunity to be hard workers for the Lord. We may be tired because we've done great things for His kingdom in His name. Living for God definitely can wear on us, but that is no reason to give up. When we are weary, that is the moment we get to and have to lean upon the Lord for strength. Oftentimes, when we're at our end, God begins. We may wear down, but we will not burn out as long as we are gaining our momentum from our Lord. Keep on running your race by being focused on doing the Father's work.

> We are blessed to be participants in the eternal work that God is doing on this earth.

The purpose of our existence is to further eternity by sharing the gospel. The Bible doesn't say that working for the Lord, sharing the gospel and doing everything unto Him, is easy and effortless. One of the first times I went out street witnessing with a church group, a man came up fuming and asked who he could talk to. Everyone else in the group was talking to someone so I was the only one available. I told him I would talk to him. He looked at me and said, "I am Jesus Christ." I was a bit afraid because this guy looked like if I said the wrong thing he would answer me with a fist in my face! It was quite an introduction for me as far as street witnessing goes! Peering into the lives of those in the Bible who lived for the Lord, there is a commonality. They all had major trials and multiple tribulations. Just thinking of what Jesus alone faced is enough to give us a glimpse into what we will face as believers. Trials and tribulations are part of doing kingdom work and that's a fact. If you are not facing pushback for living for the Lord, you may not be getting the gospel out. Now is not the time to stay and remain quiet. It's time to have a sense of urgency when it comes to proclaiming the truth in this lie-infested world. The important thing to remember is that God will get us through any opposition, hardship and difficulty. Trials will come, but when our motivation is to simply serve the Lord, we will push through and get through every obstacle.

I believe you and I are called to make kingdom work a priority. You are not alive to just go through the motions and live monotonously with the goal of just surviving. God is calling you to make Him your motivation and your passion. There is so much to do in the name of the Lord and now is the time to do it. You and I will not live forever, so may we forge ahead in the faith and seek first His work and His ways. May our motivation be to see God move as we act as His hands and feet on this earth. Follow Jesus' example in seeking God and implementing His will on this earth. Working for the Lord is worth every trial. Let's go!

DAY 30

GO ALL OUT

> *"Go therefore and make disciples of all the nations, baptizing them in the name of the Father and of the Son and of the Holy Spirit."* (Matthew 28:19)

As God grows your faith, you are called to teach those who are newer in the faith. Does that sound scary? It shouldn't be because new believers are longing and desiring to know more and learn as much as they can. You have the divine opportunity to disciple or pour wisdom into those who surround you. What you are blessed to learn needs to be relayed to those who want to learn.

Have you ever started a project and left it undone? Is it still in your garage or spare room, waiting for some attention? We all start projects and hobbies, but we don't follow through until completion. It was a good idea and so we went with it, only to realize it was too much work, we didn't have enough time, or we just thought it would be better than it turned out to be. Generally speaking, God calls believers to get out and share the light of the gospel with this dark world. When we go all out for the Lord, we are saying yes to the Great Commission. When we hear Sunday sermons or podcasts, we may get fired up to get out in our community and share the good news. But oftentimes the fire dies down when we go on to the next task. How do we follow through with sharing the gospel and getting the truth out? One way is to remember that sharing the gospel isn't a burden; it's a great blessing and a privilege. Someone at some point shared with you and they were not timid. Aren't you grateful they were bold in telling you about Jesus? I am so thankful for those people God placed in my life to share the truth with me. Making disciples starts with honestly dispensing truth to this world so as to make an impact in the name of the Lord.

> We are not called to be silent cowards; we are called to be brave and bold.

We are called to create a spiritual atmosphere. I know a missionary in Uganda who, when mission teams come over, he makes sure to tell them, "Keep it spiritual." If someone was playing secular music, he would tell them to please only play worship songs. If someone was reading a novel, he would encourage them to read the Bible. This may sound strict but groups who visit his ministry in Uganda on mission trips really appreciate his heart! He wants them to be aware that what they are doing is for God's kingdom and there cannot be any distractions. In our lives I believe we should keep it spiritual. Jesus walked on this earth, met with sinners and left them thinking about the eternal aspects of life. He did not get caught up in earthly affairs, gossip or petty drama. Instead, Jesus was consumed by the things of God and relayed that reality every place He visited. May we be all about the spiritual side of life on planet Earth. Everywhere we go in this life we are blessed to be examples of the Lord. We can make a difference by simply enacting God's Word in everyday life and be the people with boots on the ground, doing the work that has lasting impact.

You are called to make an impact in this world. You have the great privilege to proclaim the truth that has radically changed your life, so don't hold back. God wants to use you in mighty ways and as you step out in faith, the Lord will enable you to annihilate inhibition and put passivity to death. Be bold for the Lord—give them Jesus and don't be afraid! Today's the day and now's the time!

CONCLUSION

My desire was to write a devotional, each day reflecting on the words of Jesus. Words are incredibly important and life-altering. They have started wars and ended lives. Words can break down or they can build up. God's Word has given truth to countless people and saved many souls. Jesus is our example of how to live and what actions to take. As you continue seeking Him, I pray that God would use you in mighty and magnificent ways! You have a calling and now is the time to live it out! You are saved and now it's time to be set to work. Ready, set, go!

www.ingramcontent.com/pod-product-compliance
Lightning Source LLC
Chambersburg PA
CBHW060336050426
42449CB00011B/2771